THE HOW AND WHY WONDER® BOOK OF
ROCKS AND MINERALS

By Nelson W. Hyler
Illustrated by Kenyon Shannon

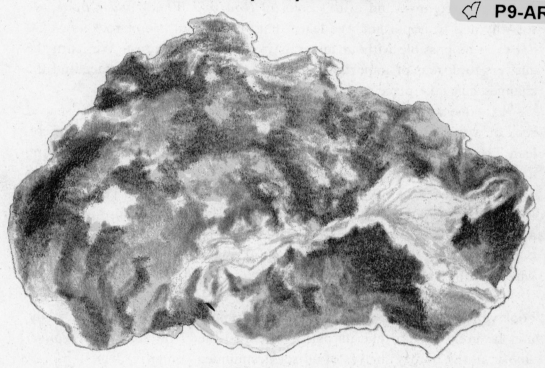

Edited under the supervision of

Dr. Paul E. Blackwood
Washington, D. C.

Text and illustrations approved by

Oakes A. White
Brooklyn Children's Museum
Brooklyn, New York

⊠ ALLAN PUBLISHERS, INC.
Exclusive Distributors

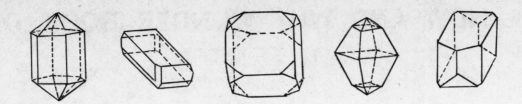

INTRODUCTION

In an age of rockets and missiles, the study of rocks and minerals is no less important — and in this colorful *How and Why Wonder®Book,* we see why it is so important. We learn that our modern age of rockets would not even be possible without minerals from the earth's crust. We learn the answers to dozens of important questions about the earth's surface and the changes that take place in it.

Anyone who has ever picked up a rounded pebble, a curiously shaped rock or a sparkling gem and handled it with wonder knows the urge to collect. The chances are that almost everyone who has walked in a field, along a stream or in a park has pocketed a sample of rock or mineral to examine and enjoy later. What is it? How was it made? Is it valuable? This *How and Why Wonder®Book* about rocks and minerals is useful because it helps to answer these and other questions. In addition, it tells how to start and how to organize a rock collection. It is a helpful guide for parents and children who want to study rocks together.

Scientists who study the earth's surface are called geologists, and this book will help children explore the big questions which geologists are studying. It surely should take its place with the other *How and Why Wonder®Books* on the library shelves of all science-minded young readers.

Paul E. Blackwood

Dr. Blackwood is a professional employee in the U. S. Office of Education. This book was edited by him in his private capacity and no official support or endorsement by the Office of Education is intended or should be inferred.

CONTENTS

THE WORLD OF ROCKS AND MINERALS

What is our earth made of?

ALMOST all of the earth — the hills, the mountains, the ground itself — is made of rocks and minerals.

There are many different kinds, and it would take a long time just to write down all their names. Yet, most of the rocks and minerals on earth are very common.

Sand is a common mineral. It is common because it is found everywhere.

Water is another common mineral. We find it in the streams and in the rivers. It fills the lakes and the seas. Most of the earth is covered with water. The great oceans of the world, together with the streams, rivers and lakes, cover about three-fourths of the surface of the world.

Mixed up in these waters are other minerals. We cannot see them by looking into the water, but they are there just the same. These minerals have been dissolved in the water.

Water is very important because we cannot live without it. It helps to make up an important part of our earth.

LEARNING ABOUT OUR WORLD

Why do we study about rocks and minerals?

WE LIVE in a wonderful world. It is full of interesting things and it is fun to learn about things.

Almost all of our world — even the inside of the world — is made of rocks and minerals. We study them to learn about our world.

Every day we use something made of rocks or minerals. But often they have been changed. They do not look the same.

Glass does not look like sand. Yet glass is made from sand. The ink that printed the letters on this page was made from minerals. We study about rocks and minerals to learn about the things we use every day.

Many people earn their living by working with rocks and minerals, making them into many different things we use. Some people have fun just looking for and finding rocks. It is important to learn about rocks and minerals so we can learn to live better.

We study about rocks and minerals to learn about our world, to learn about the things we use, and to learn to earn a livelihood.

ROCKS

What is a rock?

ROCKS are made of minerals. A few are made of just one mineral, but most of them are made of many minerals. There are many kinds of rocks.

Very small rocks are called sand. Very small sand is like sugar or salt. The individual grains are so small that they are hard to see.

Rocks bigger than sand have other names, like pebbles, or stones. Big rocks are called boulders. Some of them may be as big as a house.

Rocks are big and little. They have different shapes and sizes. Rocks are sometimes round like a ball, or square like a block.

Rocks are of many colors. You can find red rocks, blue rocks and yellow rocks. Often rocks are made of mixed colors. When you look, you can find them of almost every color.

THE SEASHORE, AT LOW TIDE, SHOWING SAND, ROCKS OF DIFFERENT SIZES, AND ROCK CLIFFS IN THE BACKGROUND

**Are rocks
found everywhere?**

ROCKS are found almost everywhere. The most common place is outdoors on the ground. Most of the ground is made up of big and little rocks.

Rocks are found at the seashore. Even the tiny pieces of sand are countless little rocks that make up the beach. The waves of the ocean wash and roll the sand around.

Outdoors you can find many rocks. You can find rocks in the hills, in the valleys and in rivers and streams.

The rocks in the rivers and streams are smooth and round. The water moves along and pushes them around. The rocks then become smooth and round by rubbing and bumping against each other.

In this way sharp rocks are broken into smaller rocks and in time are made smooth and round. Rocks are being changed all the time by moving water.

MINERALS ARE ALL AROUND US — AT HOME, IN SCHOOL AND OUTDOORS. THE KITCHEN IN YOUR HOME USUALLY HAS MANY THINGS MADE OF MINERALS.

MINERALS

What is a mineral?

A MINERAL is a chemical element or a combination of chemical elements. Minerals are all around us and they are easily found almost everywhere. In fact, it may be said that anything that is not an animal or a vegetable is a mineral.

You should be able to look around as you read this book and see some of these minerals. Can you see a window? The glass is a mineral. Can you see a dish? Can you see any kitchen pots and pans? These and other household articles are made out of minerals, too.

A good part of your wooden pencil is made of minerals. The part that makes the black mark is made of graphite — a mineral. The metal part that holds the eraser is made up of minerals, too, as is the paint on the pencil.

Almost all minerals are solids, but water is a liquid mineral. It is made up of two chemical elements — oxygen and hydrogen.

Some other minerals are clay, chalk and oil. Metals, such as iron, silver and gold are minerals, too. Scientists have found about 2,000 different specimens.

Where can you find minerals?

SOME minerals are found on top of the ground. Others are dug up from under the ground.

Many people go around looking for minerals. Prospectors are men who look for valuable minerals. In many places they have found large deposits. Then a mine may be started, if enough is found in one place. The mineral is then taken out of the mine and sold.

A mine where iron is found is called an iron mine and the mineral taken out is named iron ore. The word "ore" usually refers to any natural material which contains a valuable metal. A gold mine has gold ore and a lead mine has lead ore.

In many cases, more than one kind of ore is found together. Often, for example, silver and lead ores are close together.

All minerals do not come from mines. Some of our important minerals come from the sea. Salt is an important mineral. You use salt in your food. Salt is found both in the sea and on the land.

OPEN PIT IRON MINE

VOLCANOES

THE BEGINNING OF A VOLCANO

THE START OF A LITTLE VOLCANO

What is an active volcano? AN ACTIVE volcano is one that is said to be "erupting." It shoots out steam, ash and hot rocks. Such a volcano is working and it is active.

Millions of years ago there were many active volcanoes. They were working in many places. Some were working here in America.

A volcano begins deep down in the earth, where it is very hot. It is so hot that the rock has turned into magma — a name for very hot rock.

Deep in the earth there is much hot magma, which is sometimes pushed upward by pressure from the heavy rocks all around it. Finally the hot magma reaches the top of the ground. Here it breaks a little crack or hole in the earth. Steam, ashes and hot rocks come out.

Loud noises come from it as the rocks are blown out. The rocks pile up around the hole and the pile begins to form a cone about the crack in the earth. The cone is made up of rock, ashes and material thrown out of the volcano.

This is the beginning of a little volcano. Day after day it works and grows.

A DORMANT VOLCANO

AN OLD VOLCANO FORMED INTO A MOUNTAIN

The rocks and ashes grow into a big hill. More ashes and hot rocks come out of the hole at the top of it. Another name for this hill is a volcano.

Sometimes the volcano pours out lava. Lava is very hot and is made of hot melted rock, which is also called molten rock.

The old volcano has worked for many years. It has built a large mountain and made some smaller hills close by. The volcano has turned the flat land into hills and mountains.

Other volcanoes have been working, too, helping to build up the land.

Volcanoes that worked many millions of years ago are no longer active. Only the hills and mountains they built long ago remain to tell us that they once existed.

When a volcano has not erupted for a long time, it is dormant. This kind of volcano is known to be inactive. If it is inactive for a very long time, it may be considered dead. Then the volcano is said to be extinct.

What is an igneous rock?

IGNEOUS is the name of one of the three big groups of rocks. Igneous rocks were made in a special way.

The word igneous means made from fire or heat. Therefore, all igneous rocks have been formed by heat.

Deep down in the earth it is very hot. The rocks and minerals there are very hot. The heat has helped to change these rocks and minerals into molten rock, called magma.

BASALT CLIFF

When the magma comes up to the surface of the earth, it cools off and becomes hard. The cold magma, hardened into rock, is called igneous rock. There are many different kinds of igneous rocks, but all of them have come from the magma found deep in the earth.

Sometimes the magma does not get all the way up to the earth's surface. It cools underneath the ground, turning into rock before it gets to the surface. This kind of igneous rock is called granite.

Huge rocks are formed under the ground in this manner. Sometimes the rocks made in this way are several miles long and almost as wide and deep.

GRANITE

THE THREE BIG GROUPS OF ROCKS

Where do igneous rocks come from?

A GOOD place to find igneous rocks is near old volcanoes. These rocks were made when the volcanoes were still active. Today you can still find the rocks they made.

Many different kinds of rocks are found near the old volcanoes. Lava is one. It is a common igneous rock.

Lava in the form of molten rock pours out of a crack in the side of a volcano. It runs steaming down the side of the volcano and over everything in its path.

RIGHT: AN ERUPTING VOLCANO SHOWING MOLTEN ROCK AND LAVA FLOWING DOWN ITS SIDE. BELOW: IGNEOUS DUMP ROCK FROM VOLCANOES.

In time, the molten lava cools and hardens, turning into igneous rock. The name, lava, can mean the molten rock or even the cold hard rock.

Long ago there were many volcanoes in the western states and some in a few of the eastern states. They were active for many years, throwing out ashes, cinders, rocks and dust. Year after year they worked, building the land higher and higher.

If you live in the West, you can still see where the volcanoes once were active. Today they are extinct. Around and about them you will find many kinds of igneous rocks.

GRANITE is one of our most common igneous rocks, made deep under the ground.

Granite is made of quartz, feldspar and mica. These are all minerals. Quartz and feldspar are light-colored. They make granite a light-colored rock. The little bits of mica in granite make the dark spots.

Granite may be colored red, pink, yellow or brown. Often it is a mixture of colors in between.

GRANITE

DIORITE is an igneous rock. It is made like granite, but is much darker in color. It is darker than granite because it has no white quartz in it.

Diorite is made of dark minerals — dark feldspars and hornblende.

DIORITE

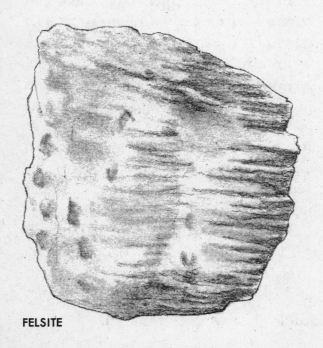

FELSITE

FELSITE rocks are made from fast-cooling lava. The lava cools too fast to turn into granite or basalt. The lava cools too slowly to make obsidian, another kind of igneous rock. It cools just right and turns into felsite.

Felsite rocks are usually made from light-colored lavas. These rocks are often colored light gray, green, yellow or even red.

BASALT is a rock that comes from volcanoes. Sometimes the lava from a volcano is a very dark color. As this dark lava slowly cools, it turns into a black rock called basalt.

Basalt is a very useful igneous rock. It is crushed and sold to make many useful things. Basalt is used in sidewalks, buildings and roads, just like granite.

This kind of rock was formed in giant sheets when the ancient volcanoes poured out huge flows of lava that cooled faster than the granite-forming magmas.

BASALT

OBSIDIAN is another igneous rock made by volcanoes. When lava flows out of the volcano, it often cools very fast and forms a rock called obsidian. This rock looks just like colored glass. It is really natural glass and is found in many colors.

Indians found obsidian very useful. They made the tips of their arrows and spears out of it. The way in which this rock breaks apart makes it easy to shape arrow and spear points.

Can you tell how the igneous rocks you have just read about were made?

Granite and diorite were formed when the magma did not reach the surface of the earth. This magma cooled very slowly deep under the earth's surface.

Basalt was made when the magma reached the surface. This magma came out of the earth and we call it lava. The lava cooled into basalt.

Felsite formed from faster cooling lava than basalt. But the fastest cooling lava of all turned into glass. This natural glass we call obsidian.

INDIANS MADE THE TIPS OF THEIR SPEARS AND ARROWS OUT OF OBSIDIAN.

15

HEAVY CRANES ARE USED BY WORKERS IN QUARRIES TO LIFT BIG ROCKS. IN THIS GRANITE QUARRY, A MAN GUIDES THE MOVEMENT OF A ROCK WHICH HAS BEEN RAISED UP BY A CRANE.

ROCK QUARRIES

What is a quarry?

A QUARRY is a large open hole in the ground or the side of a hill. It is a place where rocks and stones are dug out.

There are many kinds of rock quarries. One kind will have granite rocks. Another will have sandstone and there are some quarries of marble, too.

Big machines help the workers take the rock out of a granite quarry. The big rocks are used to build many things, but most of the time the builders need more small rocks than big rocks.

Rock-crushing machines take the big rocks and break them into smaller pieces. These small pieces of broken rock are called crushed rock or gravel, which is used to build new roads.

Rock is heavy and expensive to move a long way. Therefore, we find rock quarries close to big cities or new roads where lots of crushed rock is used for construction purposes.

EROSION

Does the earth wear out?

VOLCANOES are land builders. They help to make the land higher. But the land does not stay built up. It keeps wearing away. Day after day and year after year, the wind and the water help to wear away the land.

The wind may blow dirt, sand and soil into a nearby stream. The stream carries the dirt, sand and soil to the sea. Day after day the earth is washed away by running water.

You may have seen a muddy stream or river. It was carrying the earth toward the sea. This is the way the wind and the water are taking away the earth.

Not all streams lead to the sea. Some end in lakes or other streams. These streams carry material into the lakes. In time the lake fills up with mud, dirt, sand and the like. When this happens, the lake turns into a shallow marsh. In time the marsh may dry up. This is another place from which the wind and water may take away the land.

When the land is being moved by the wind or water, we say it is eroding. The process of erosion is going on all of the time. It may be helpful, but more often it is harmful in destroying much valuable land.

ON SEACOASTS, OCEAN WAVES ERODE THE LAND. THE WAVES CARRY LOOSE BITS OF ROCK. THESE BITS OF ROCK, PLUS THE FORCE OF THE WAVES AGAINST THE LAND, WEAR AWAY THE EARTH.

SEDIMENTARY ROCKS

Are there rocks under the water?

STIR up a handful of dirt in a glass of water. At first the water will be cloudy. But if the water is left alone, the dirt will settle to the bottom of the glass. In time the water will be clear again.

The dirt that has settled to the bottom of the glass is called sediment. From this word comes the name sedimentary, the name for the second big group of rocks.

This kind of rock was formed by sediment from rivers and streams. Every day the streams and rivers bring more and more mud, sand and rock to the seas. These settle to the bottom and are called sediment.

The big rocks settle first. They sink first because they are bigger and heavier. Next the sand and then the mud sinks to the bottom of the sea. In this way different layers are built up. The layers build up on the sea bottom year after year until they are very thick.

BODIES OF WATER HOLD MUD, SAND AND ROCKS, AS WELL AS LIVING THINGS, INCLUDING PLANTS AND SEA ANIMALS. MANY OBJECTS SINK IN THE WATER — SOME TO THE VERY BOTTOM, OTHERS ONLY PARTWAY. IN TIME, THERE ARE LAYERS OF ROCK, SAND AND MUD IN THE WATER.

MUD

SAND

ROCK

VOLCANIC TUFF IS SEDIMENTARY ROCK. TUFF IS COMPOSED OF MANY LAYERS OF VOLCANIC ASHES AND DUST. THESE LAYERS BUILT UP AROUND ACTIVE VOLCANOES.

The weight of the layers of sand and water above press down on the bottom layer of sand. This bottom layer begins to change.

Each tiny grain of sand begins to stick to another one. The sand grains change into stone. Because the stone is made from sand, we call it sandstone. Sandstone is a sedimentary rock.

Most sedimentary rock is made under the water in lakes or seas and in the oceans. But sometimes sedimentary rock is made on dry land!

For instance, long ago, many volcanoes blew out ashes and volcanic dust which settled around them. Year after year the layers built up. In time another kind of rock was made — sedimentary rock called volcanic tuff.

In the West, large areas are covered with this kind of rock. The different layers are of different colors, making a colorful sedimentary rock.

VOLCANIC LAYERS

How are rocks made?

NOT ALL sedimentary rocks were made from dirt and sand that came down the river. Some were made from the shells of sea animals and plants.

Millions of animals live in the sea. Some of them build a hard shell which is made of lime, and this protects the animal living inside. Clams and snails live in shells.

Some plants have shells, too. A diatom is a tiny plant that lives in a shell. Millions and millions of tiny shelled diatoms live in the sea.

When a plant or animal dies, its shell sinks to the bottom of the sea. After many years, millions of dead shells pile up on the bottom of the sea. Again, the top layer pushes down on the bottom layers. The shells in the bottom layer are pushed close together.

The weight of the shells on top changes the bottom layer of shells. The shell layer at the bottom turns into stone. The name of this stone is limestone, which is another kind of sedimentary rock.

Look again at the word limestone. Do you see that the first part of the word says lime? This tells us what the rock is made of. The last part of the word tells us the lime has turned into stone.

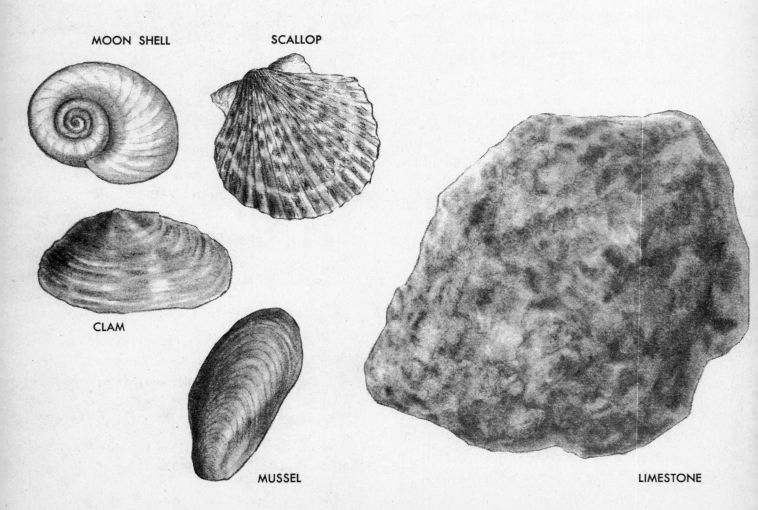

MOON SHELL

SCALLOP

CLAM

MUSSEL

LIMESTONE

Where are sedimentary rocks found?

SEDIMENTARY rocks were formed under the seas and oceans. The sedimentary rocks built up higher and higher in some places. This made the sea bottom rise higher and higher.

Millions of years went by. In some places the sea bottom rose slowly. If it rose high enough, it came out of the water.

The land that came out of the water was made of sediment. Below the top layers of sediment were sedimentary rocks. You can see these rocks today near the seashore.

NEAR THE SEASHORE, YOU CAN SEE SEDIMENTARY ROCK. LAYERS OF SEDIMENT DEPOSITS IN THE WATER ROSE HIGHER AND HIGHER. AFTER MANY YEARS, SEDIMENTARY ROCK EMERGED FROM THE WATER.

SEDIMENTARY ROCK THAT CAME OUT OF THE WATER OFTEN ROSE TO GREAT HEIGHT. YOU CAN SEE HOW LAYERS OF SEDIMENT WERE BUILT UP AS YOU DRIVE ALONG HIGHWAYS WHICH CUT THROUGH HILLS MADE OF SEDIMENTARY ROCK.

Wherever you find land that was once under water, you are almost sure to find sedimentary rock.

Roads are often cut through hills. If the hill is made of sedimentary rock, it will show the layers. You can usually find sedimentary rocks in hills that are layered.

Sedimentary rocks are very common and may be found almost everywhere. The midwestern part of our country is covered with sedimentary rocks. Large areas of the East are made of this type of rock. The West also has its share of sedimentary deposited rock.

CONGLOM-ERATE is a sedimentary rock. It is made of a mixture of smooth round stones and pebbles. The larger stones in a conglomerate rock are held together by another kind of stone, either limestone or sandstone.

Conglomerate rock is made in old streams and river beds. The large stones are washed down the stream. Then, in a quiet pool, the rocks sink to the bottom and pile up.

More rocks and sand continue to pile up in the old stream bed. In time the big and little rocks become changed into conglomerate rock.

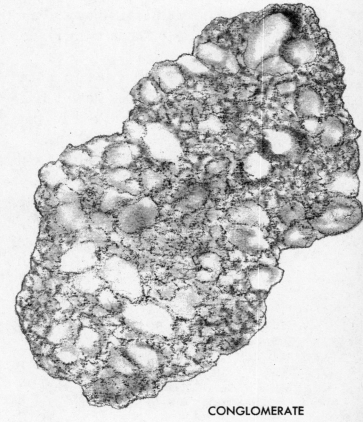

CONGLOMERATE

SANDSTONE

SANDSTONE is a very useful sedimentary rock. It is used in walls and buildings, because it is strong and easy to quarry. After it has been taken from the quarry, it is cut into blocks and used in the building of things.

There are many different colors of sandstone. Brown is common. In some places so much sandstone is colored brown it is called brownstone. You can also find yellow-colored, gray-colored and red-colored sandstones.

SHALE

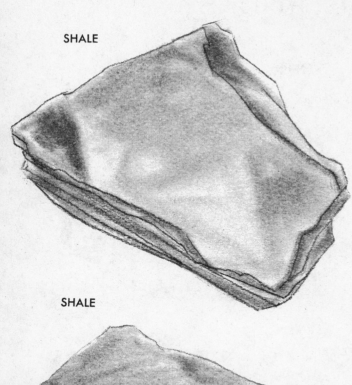

SHALE

LIMESTONE is a sedimentary rock that forms only under water. It takes millions of years to make a lot of limestone. Some deposits of limestone are thousands of feet thick!

Pure limestone is clean and white. But often other things get mixed into the limestone that may change its color. When a little bit of iron gets mixed into it, the white limestone changes to yellow or brown. Other materials can change the color of limestone to green, gray, black and many other colors.

DOLOMITE

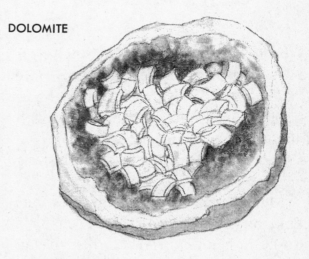

SHALE is made from fine silt and mud. Another name for it is mudstone. Yet, sometimes it is so soft, it is not like a stone at all.

Most rocks do not have any odor, but wet shale does. It smells like damp earth.

You can find shales of many different colors. Red, brown and gray are common colors of shale. The color, of course, depends upon the color of the mud or fine silt from which the shale was made.

DOLOMITE is another kind of limestone made under the sea. It is usually white or light-colored. One kind of dolomite breaks up easily. This kind looks just like white rice!

METAMORPHIC ROCKS

LIMESTONE

MARBLE

SHALE

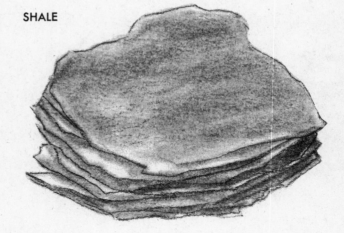

SLATE

Why do rocks have different shapes and colors? THE NAME metamorphic means "to have been changed." This name is used to tell about rocks that have been changed in some way. This is the third and last big group of rocks.

Metamorphic rocks began as one kind of rock and later were changed into another kind. All of them began once as igneous or sedimentary rocks. The new rocks do not look the same, for in becoming metamorphic rocks their structure and often their color change.

Sedimentary rocks are formed deep under the seas. After they have been formed, they may become very hot. Heat helps to change sedimentary rocks.

The weight of the rocks and water on top of the sedimentary rocks is very great. The heavy weight or pressure also helps to change the sedimentary rocks. Heat and pressure together change the sedimentary rocks into metamorphic rocks.

When limestone is changed, it turns into marble. If shale is changed, it turns into slate. Both marble and slate are metamorphic rocks.

THE HEAT AND HEAVY WEIGHT, OR PRESSURE, ON SEDIMENTARY AND IGNEOUS ROCKS HELP TO CHANGE THEM INTO METAMORPHIC ROCKS. AS A VOLCANO PUSHES ITS WAY UP THROUGH THE EARTH, GREAT HEAT IS CREATED. AS THE VOLCANO PASSES THROUGH A SEDIMENTARY LAYER, THE HEAT CHANGES THE SEDIMENTARY ROCK INTO METAMORPHIC ROCK.

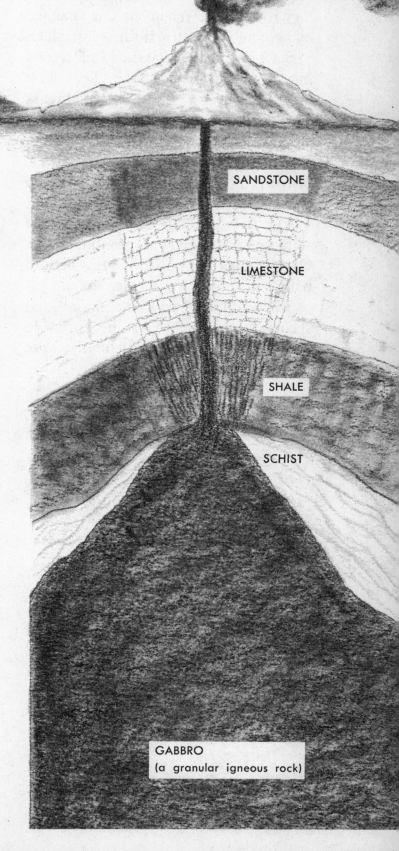

SANDSTONE

LIMESTONE

SHALE

SCHIST

GABBRO
(a granular igneous rock)

Where do metamorphic rocks come from?

SEDIMENTARY rocks are made deep under the seas and ocean bottoms. Sometimes a sea goes dry. The land moves up and the sedimentary rocks are exposed.

In time the wind and rain wear down the top layers of rock. Then another kind of rock is exposed. The rock exposed is metamorphic rock.

To find metamorphic rock, you must visit a place where the land has been wearing down for many years. There are places in the eastern United States and a few in the West where one can see this kind of rock. There are also many metamorphic rocks far north in Canada.

Sometimes metamorphic rocks can be found where old volcanoes once stood. The red hot lava from them often changed other rocks into metamorphic rocks.

This type of metamorphic rock could occur where the volcano pushed its way up through the earth, passing through a sediment layer on the way. Here the heat helped to change the sedimentary rock into metamorphic rock.

Are there many kinds of metamorphic rocks?

SLATE is a metamorphic rock made from the sedimentary rock shale. When shale is changed by heat and pressure, it turns into slate.

Slate and shale have the same colors, but they do not look alike. They look different because of how they break. The way that they break helps to tell them apart.

Slate breaks into smooth flat sheets of rock. You can split it into very thin pieces, which make fine steppingstones.

The finest blackboards are made of slate that has been split into thin sheets. One side is then polished very smooth before it is used for a blackboard.

Shale will not break into smooth flat sheets of rock. It breaks only into odd shapes. This stone has little use because of the way in which it breaks.

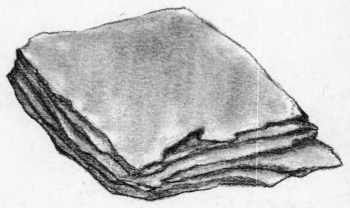

SLATE

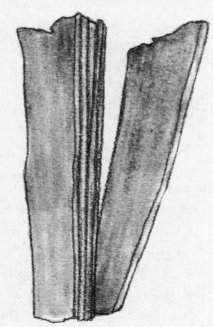

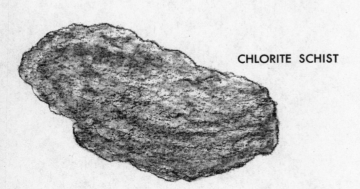

CHLORITE SCHIST

QUARTZ SCHIST

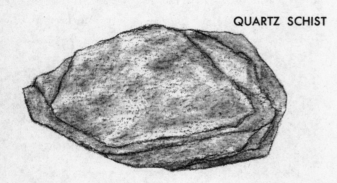

SCHIST is a metamorphic rock made from mudstone or shale. Rock must be changed many times in order to make schist.

As schist is made, some of the minerals in it change. These minerals then become mica and all are turned the same way. The little bits of mica make the schist shine and sparkle.

SERPENTINE

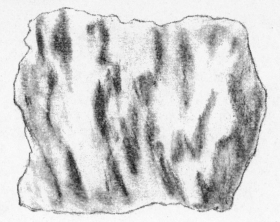

BLACK MARBLE

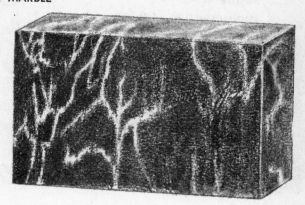

SERPENTINE is a metamorphic rock often colored green. Some serpentine rocks are light green and some are dark green. This stone is slippery to touch. It feels as if it were covered with wax or soap.

When this rock is exposed to the weather, it soon breaks down and crumbles away.

WHITE MARBLE

QUARTZITE

QUARTZITE is a very hard metamorphic rock made from hard sandstone.

Pressure and heat changed the sandstone into hard quartzite. Some quartzite is colored like sandstone. These colors are yellow, brown, pink and red.

MARBLE is a metamorphic rock. It comes from limestone that has been changed by heat and pressure. Marble is made-over limestone.

Marble is often many different colors. You can find white marble or black marble or just about any color in between. Often the marble is striped or marked with several colors. Minerals, or impurities, in the marble change its color.

This stone is used in some of the great public buildings in our country. Many beautiful monuments are made with this useful stone.

AMAZONITE (or Amazon stone)

Triclinic System

EPIDOTE

Monoclinic System

SULPHUR

Orthorhombic System

CALCITE

Hexagonàl System

RUTILE

Tetragonal System

HALITE (salt)

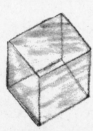

Cubic System

CRYSTALS

**What is
a crystal?**

THERE are non-living substances which grow into bodies of various shapes. They grow by adding on more layers of the same substance, keeping the same shape at all times. These bodies of various shapes are called crystals. Most solid substances, like minerals, are crystalline; that is, they are made up of crystals. So a crystal is really another form of rocks and minerals, except that the word "crystal" tells us that the rock or mineral is of a certain shape.

These different crystal shapes, which help us to tell the minerals apart, are grouped into six main kinds or systems: Cubic System, Tetragonal System, Hexagonal System, Orthorhombic System, Monoclinic System and Triclinic System. Examples of the six different shapes may be seen in the crystal forms shown on this page.

When minerals are first formed, they often turn into crystals. It takes a long time to make big crystals, but some little crystals can be made in two days.

How can you make a crystal?

HERE is a way to make some crystals of your own. Salt crystals are easy to make.

Stir three tablespoons full of salt into a cup of warm water. As you stir the water, the salt will disappear. In a few minutes you will not be able to see the salt crystals. They have disappeared into the water.

Next pour the salty water into a pie pan. Set the pan where it will be warm. Salt crystals will grow faster in a warm place.

Now you must wait for the water to evaporate. This may take a few days. Little by little the water will disappear.

Every day look at the pan of salt water. Soon white crystals will begin to form around the edge of the pan. The white crystals are made of salt.

Sugar crystals can be made in the same way. Even bigger crystals than sugar or salt can be made by dissolving alum crystals. When they turn back into crystals again, you will be surprised at their size. You can buy alum at any drugstore for a few cents.

MINERAL FOODS

Where does the salt we eat come from?

MUCH OF our salt is made near the sea-shore, in large flat ponds filled with sea water. This water contains lots of salt.

Day after day the hot sun shines and warms the sea water in the pond. Warm sea water helps the salt crystals to form.

As each day goes by, a little more water disappears by evaporation. Salt crystals form in the water that is left.

After many days, the sea water is all gone and only the salt is left behind. The salt has formed as white crystals on the bottom of the dry pond.

When the pond is dry, workmen can gather the salt. The salt is put into little boxes for us to use. Everyone uses salt crystals left behind by the sea water.

Many years ago salt was difficult to get in some countries. Workmen have even been paid wages with salt, instead of money!

This kind of salt has another name — halite. Halite is the mineral name for salt, but most of the time halite is just called salt.

SALT PONDS USED IN THE EVAPORATION OF SEA WATER

Can we eat minerals?

YOU MAY be surprised to learn that every day you eat many different minerals besides salt. These minerals are very helpful to you.

Water is a very common mineral. It is the most important mineral you use. Some of it is in the food you eat. Other water is in the milk you drink. Your body needs some water every day.

You only need to eat very tiny amounts of the other minerals which are found in foods. They cannot be seen because there are only tiny bits of them. But they are very important.

Iron is an important mineral used to make cars and other things. It is also a mineral you need to eat. It is found in eggs and liver. Calcium is a mineral found in cheese, and it helps to make strong bones. Iodine is a mineral needed to keep your body healthy. Iodine is often mixed with the salt you eat.

All of these minerals and many more are found in the food you eat. You need to eat many different kinds of food because each kind has different minerals. They help you to build a healthy body.

EGGS AND MEAT (iron)

CHEESE (calcium)

SALT (iodine)

FISH (phosphorus)

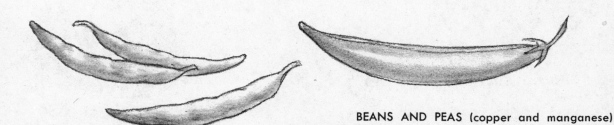

BEANS AND PEAS (copper and manganese)

31

ROCK-FORMING MINERALS

What are some of the rock-forming minerals?

ROCKS are made from one or more kinds of minerals. Granite is a rock made from three kinds of minerals — quartz, feldspar and mica.

Quartz, feldspar and mica are rock-forming minerals. They are called that because they make rocks, like granite.

QUARTZ is one of the most common rock-forming minerals and is found in all the big groups of rocks — igneous, sedimentary and metamorphic rocks.

Some quartz is colorless, like ice. Other colors are white, pink, violet and gray. Sometimes the dark-colored quartz is called smoky quartz. It looks like the color of dark smoke.

You can find quartz very easily. The small sand grains in dirt are often quartz. Beach sand is usually full of quartz grains. It is found in most igneous rocks, often in the form of crystals.

In fact, the names of many minerals and rocks depend upon whether or not quartz is present in the sample. You should consider quartz to be one of the most important rock-forming minerals.

ROCK CRYSTAL IN DRUSY QUARTZ

CITRINE QUARTZ

SMOKY QUARTZ

ROSE QUARTZ

AMETHYST QUARTZ

FELDSPAR is a very common rock-forming mineral, like quartz. But the name feldspar is really a family name. That is, it is a name used for six or seven different feldspar minerals.

All of these feldspar minerals are much alike, sometimes so much so that it is hard to tell them apart. It is easier to just call them feldspar. So feldspar is the family name given to all of them.

Feldspar minerals occur in almost all of the igneous rocks. Often the color of the rock depends upon the color of the feldspar mixed into it.

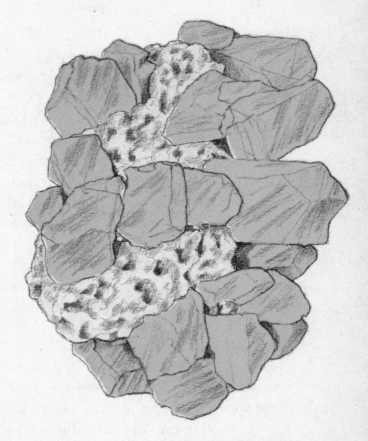

MICROCLINE FELDSPAR

GRANITE WITH PINK FELDSPAR

GRANITE WITH WHITE FELDSPAR

Feldspar may be colored white, light pink or even green. The white and pink colors are the ones you will see most often.

Granite with pink feldspar will look pink. If the feldspar is white, the granite will look white. The quartz in the granite helps to change the color, too.

As granite grows old and is exposed to the weather, it begins to fall apart. We say that it is beginning to decompose. Actually, it is the feldspar in the granite that is breaking apart. In time the wind and water help to change the feldspar into clay.

IDENTIFICATION OF ROCKS AND MINERALS

How do we begin to identify rocks and minerals?

THERE ARE several ways to identify rocks and minerals. First you will have to make some tests. These tests are easy to do and will help you to know more about rocks and minerals.

Each test you make will tell you more about your new rock, until at last you will be able to tell the rock's name.

You must not expect to be able to name every new rock or mineral at first. In the beginning you will be able to name only a few. It takes a long time to learn most of the names of the rocks and minerals.

One of the first tests you will make is to ask yourself, "Where did this rock come from?" Is it an igneous rock? Or does it look more like a sedimentary rock? It might be even a metamorphic rock!

You would first like to know what general kind of rock it is. When you know where it came from, you can often tell what general kind it is.

Once you know if it is an igneous, sedimentary or metamorphic rock, you can make some other tests.

GRANITE IS AN IGNEOUS ROCK COLORED RED, PINK, YELLOW OR BROWN. IT IS USED OFTEN IN CONSTRUCTION WORK.

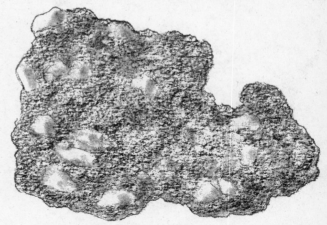

CONGLOMERATE IS A SEDIMENTARY ROCK MADE OF STONES AND PEBBLES, HELD TOGETHER BY LIMESTONE OR SANDSTONE. LIMESTONE IS OFTEN WHITE AND SANDSTONE IS USUALLY BROWN.

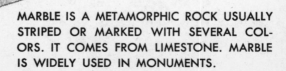

MARBLE IS A METAMORPHIC ROCK USUALLY STRIPED OR MARKED WITH SEVERAL COLORS. IT COMES FROM LIMESTONE. MARBLE IS WIDELY USED IN MONUMENTS.

IN THE FIELD, THERE ARE SOME SIMPLE WAYS TO TEST THE HARDNESS OF ROCKS AND MINERALS.

YOUR FINGERNAIL CAN SCRATCH TWO MINERALS — TALC AND GYPSUM.

A PENNY IS HARDER THAN YOUR FINGERNAIL AND CAN SCRATCH CALCITE, AS WELL AS TALC AND GYPSUM.

THE BLADE OF A SMALL POCKET KNIFE IS HARDER THAN A PENNY. IT CAN SCRATCH FLUORITE AND APATITE, AS WELL AS THE MINERALS BELOW THEM ON THE SCALE.

HARDER MINERALS CAN SCRATCH THE SOFTER ONES, AND EACH MINERAL CAN SCRATCH ANOTHER OF ITS KIND.

How can you tell how hard a rock or mineral is?

ONE of the most important tests you can make on a specimen is to find out how hard it is. Hardness tells you how easy it is to scratch one mineral with another. Some minerals are very soft. Others are very hard.

If you know how hard or soft a specimen is, it will help you to tell it apart from other minerals.

Geologists, for a long time, have used ten minerals to test for hardness. These ten minerals are called the *Scale of Hardness* minerals.

Each mineral on the scale has a number as well as a name. You have already read about the names of some, and others will be new to you.

There are also some common things that will help you to test for hardness. One of these testers you have with you all of the time — your fingernail — which will scratch at least two minerals. A penny can also be used to scratch certain minerals, and a small pocket knife is another common tester. Its blade will scratch still other minerals. Each mineral can also scratch itself. You will read about these and others in the discussion about the *"Scale of Hardness"* minerals, beginning on the next page.

These minerals have been arranged in order. The softest mineral is number one and the hardest is number ten. Those minerals in between will vary, each higher-numbered mineral being harder than the one before.

THE SCALE OF
HARDNESS MINERALS

What are the hardness minerals?

N*UMBER 1. TALC:* Talc is a metamorphic mineral. It is the softest of the minerals in the scale. You can scratch talc with your fingernail.

Talcum powder is made from ground-up talc. Of course, the nice smell is put in after the talc is ground up.

FOLIATED TALC ON SERPENTINE

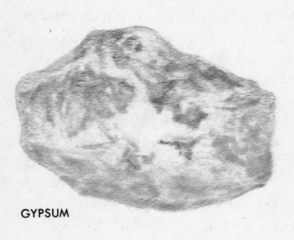

GYPSUM

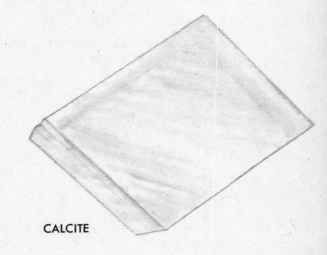

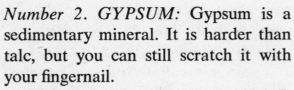

CALCITE

Number 2. GYPSUM: Gypsum is a sedimentary mineral. It is harder than talc, but you can still scratch it with your fingernail.

Gypsum may be colorless or white. It is found in huge beds in the ground where it is dug out. Gypsum is an important mineral. Plaster of Paris is made from it. Plaster wallboard is also made from gypsum. Did you know that the blackboard chalk you use in school was made from gypsum?

Number 3. CALCITE: Calcite is third in the hardness scale. It scratches talc and gypsum. You can scratch calcite with a penny.

Calcite is a colorless or white mineral. You will find it in many places and with all groups of rocks.

A special form of calcite is Iceland Spar. When you look through a clear crystal of Iceland Spar, everything suddenly looks double!

FLUORITE

FELDSPAR

Number 4. FLUORITE: This mineral is one of the most colorful of the hardness minerals. Crystals of fluorite may be white, gray, black and many other colors. They may also be colorless.

Fluorite is four on the hardness scale, but you can scratch it with a small pocket knife.

Number 6. FELDSPAR: Feldspar is about the most common mineral on the earth. When this mineral breaks up and rots, it turns into clay. Clay is found almost everywhere.

Your knife will not scratch feldspar, but the feldspar will scratch your knife!

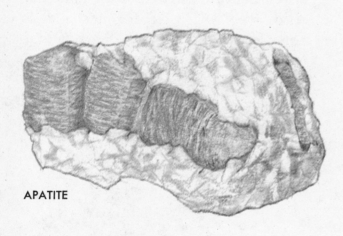

APATITE

QUARTZ

Number 5. APATITE: Apatite is another mineral that forms beautiful crystals of many different colors. Some of these colors are white, brown, green, violet, blue and yellow. Yellow is the most common color.

You can scratch apatite with a knife, too. Apatite in turn will scratch any of the hardness minerals below it. Apatite, like each of the other minerals, is able to scratch itself.

Number 7. QUARTZ: Quartz is a common mineral you have already read about. It comes in many colors. A beautiful kind of quartz is named Tiger's Eye and is used in jewelry.

Quartz sand is melted and turned into clear glass. Radios and phonographs very often have special quartz crystals in them. Quartz is very useful. It is the hardest mineral you are apt to find easily.

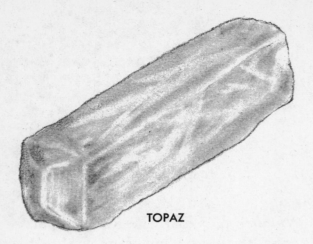

TOPAZ

Number 8. TOPAZ: Topaz is a very hard stone. It will scratch quartz or any of the other minerals below quartz. Topaz is prized as a gem stone because it is very beautiful. This stone is commonly yellow.

CORUNDUM (ruby)

Number 9. CORUNDUM: Corundum is next to the hardest mineral. Some crystals of this mineral are also gem stones. Ruby is a clear red corundum crystal. Such a crystal is quite valuable.

Ordinary corundum is crushed into small bits and made into sandpaper.

Number 10. DIAMOND: This is the hardest mineral known on earth. Nothing is harder than diamond. It is many times as hard as corundum. Clear crystals are made into jewels. Dark-colored diamonds are used to polish and cut other hard stones, as well as other diamonds, too. Diamonds are valuable because they are very hard, beautiful and rare.

These are the hardness minerals. They are all used for many things. Testing the hardness of other minerals is just one of the things for which they are used.

As you become more interested in rocks and minerals, you will want to have a set of hardness testing minerals. A set is not expensive, for most sets do not contain a diamond. Since a diamond could only test another diamond, there is little need for one in the set.

Even before you have such a set, many tests can be made with your fingernail, a penny, a pocket knife and a piece of quartz.

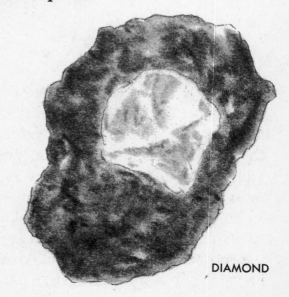

DIAMOND

SIMPLE TESTS

How can you tell what kind of rock it is?

YOU CAN test for the name of a rock or mineral with a streak plate. A streak plate is made of unglazed tile.

Many specimens leave a colored streak when they are rubbed on the streak plate. The color of the streak helps to name the rock. You can make red, blue, black and many other colored streaks. Some samples will not even make a streak!

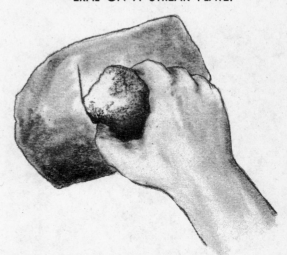

RUB THE ROCK OR THE MINERAL ON A STREAK PLATE.

THE STREAKS MADE BY THE HARDNESS MINERALS VARY FROM WHITE TO GRAY, WHILE SOME OF THE MINERALS MAKE NO STREAKS OR ARE COLORLESS. GENERALLY, NON-METALLIC MINERALS MAKE COLORLESS TO LIGHT GRAY STREAKS, AND METALLIC MINERALS MAKE DARK GRAY TO BLACK STREAKS.

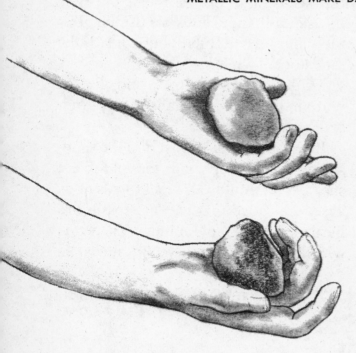

A SIMPLE WAY TO TEST ROCKS AND MINERALS FOR WEIGHT IS TO HOLD A DIFFERENT SPECIMEN IN EACH HAND. EVEN THOUGH BOTH ROCKS ARE OF THE SAME SIZE, ONE WILL WEIGH MORE THAN THE OTHER.

How can you test a rock or mineral for weight?

YOU CANNOT look at a rock or mineral and tell how heavy it is. Yet, some minerals or rocks are much heavier than others. When you pick up a sample rock, you can tell if it seems heavy or light.

When you try this with a different rock in each hand, you can tell which is the heavier. Both samples must be about the same size, of course. You will be surprised to see how easily you can tell the difference in weight between two rocks. Whether the rock is heavy or light may help to tell its name.

More advanced books will show you other ways of finding the weight of a rock or mineral.

FOSSILS

**What is
a fossil?**

A FOSSIL is the remains of some animal or plant which is no longer living. It has been dead for many years and only part of the animal or plant is left today. This part is called a fossil.

Clams often turn into fossils. Here is how this can happen.

When a clam dies, the soft parts of its body soon rot away. But the shell of the clam is very hard. It is made of calcium, like our bones, and cannot rot away. The shell sinks to the sand at the bottom of the sea.

Many years pass and other shells join the first shell. Fine sand washes over the shells and buries them. In time the sand changes into sandstone. But the shells are still there, buried with the sandstone.

Millions of years go by and the sea bottom becomes dry land. The sandstone can now be seen.

If you should dig down into the sandstone, you would find the old clam shells. You would call them fossils now. They are called that because fossils are hardened traces of animals or plants which have been preserved in the earth.

HERE ARE CLAM SHELL FOSSILS WHICH HAVE BEEN PRESERVED IN SANDSTONE.

THE WORD *FOSSIL* COMES FROM A LATIN WORD MEANING "DUG UP." THE DISCOVERY OF FOSSIL REMAINS OF ANIMALS ON LAND AND IN THE SEA HAS GIVEN SCIENTISTS MUCH INFORMATION ABOUT THE WORLD AS IT WAS MILLIONS OF YEARS AGO.

Why do we study fossils?

SOME day you may find a fossil. You will want to know its name. You may ask yourself, "Where did this come from? Is it an animal or is it a rock? How did it get here? Is it valuable?" These and many other questions may occur to you.

The scientists who search for fossils and study them are known as *paleontologists*. By learning of life and changes that occurred on earth in the past, they can supply answers for the future.

Fossils give us a record and a picture of the past that is beyond the ken of human memory. From them we can find out not only what certain plants and animals looked like, but can deduce other things. For example, by finding fossil shellfish in presently mountainous regions, we can scientifically conclude that the area was once under sea water. By finding fossils of tropical plants in Greenland, we must conclude that this land mass once had a climate quite different from what it has today.

Where are fossils found?

ONE of the best places to look for fossils is in sedimentary rocks. Soft shale and sandstone often have fossils in them. These are both sedimentary rocks.

Limestone is a sedimentary rock made up of millions of tiny shells of sea animals. Sometimes the shells of the animals can be seen in the limestone. You could think of this kind of limestone as "fossil stone."

THE SHELLS OF SEA ANIMALS CONTRIBUTE TO THE FORMATION OF LIMESTONE. LIMESTONE IS, THEREFORE, A GOOD SOURCE OF FOSSILS. NOTE THE SHELLS IN THIS STONE.

GOOD EXAMPLES OF PETRIFIED WOOD MAY BE FOUND IN THE PETRIFIED FOREST NATIONAL PARK IN THE STATE OF ARIZONA.

Trees and plants that are near lakes and streams often fall into the water. Sometimes they sink to the bottom and are buried in the soft mud. The years pass by. More mud covers the old trees. Slowly the trees change into fossils.

This takes many years to occur. But finally the tree has been changed from wood into a mineral. It is no longer made of wood, but of stone. We call this kind of stone petrified wood.

There are places in the West where whole forests of petrified trees or fossils are found. Some areas have been set aside as national or state monuments to preserve these trees and fossils from souvenir hunters. You may some day visit one of these places yourself.

RARE STONES

What makes a mineral a gem stone?

GEM stones are rare and more difficult to find than ordinary rocks. They are harder to find because there are not so many of them. If a stone is hard to find, if it is beautiful, and if it can be polished, it then becomes valuable. This kind of stone is named a gem stone.

For hundreds of years men have looked for valuable gem stones and minerals. Today other men are still hunting for new places to find gem stones.

A ruby is a beautiful red-colored gem stone. When a ruby is polished, it sparkles and shines. The color of the ruby helps to make it valuable.

Other gem stones are opals, pearls, emeralds and diamonds. Emeralds and diamonds are the most expensive and rarest gem stones. All gem stones are beautiful. Gem stones are used in jewelry. They are often set in rings.

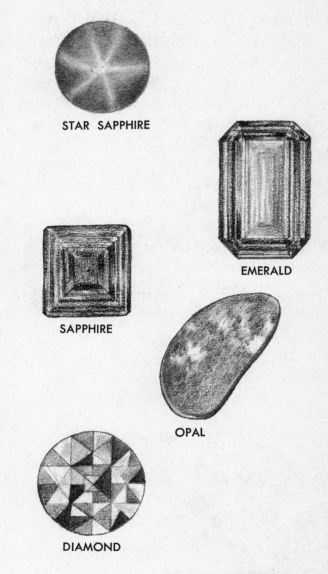

STAR SAPPHIRE

EMERALD

SAPPHIRE

OPAL

DIAMOND

RUBY

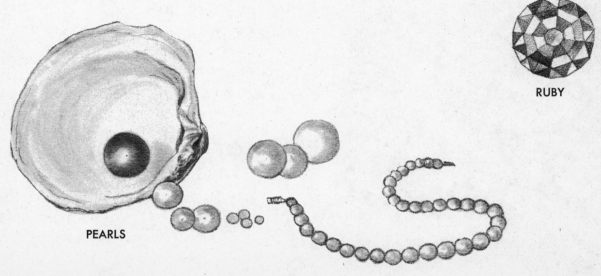

PEARLS

PUMICE

What is pumice?

PUMICE is an igneous rock. It is made by volcanoes. Sometimes the volcano throws out gobs of molten rock. Little holes grow in the rock before it cools. These holes are caused by steam or gas trapped in the molten rock. The holes in pumice look just like the holes in a loaf of bread!

Pumice is a stone that can float on water! It floats on water because it is so very light.

This stone is used to polish fine furniture and to make building materials.

PUMICE

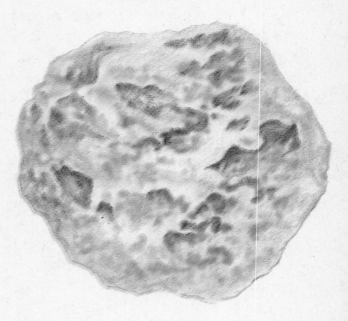

COAL

COAL

What is coal?

COAL IS A sedimentary rock that will burn. Coal burns just as wood does. It is used to build warm fires.

Coal was made millions of years ago. This rock is made from plants, and trees or ferns that lived long ago.

These trees and plants became buried just like fossils. In time they turned into coal. Coal is really the remains of many trees and plants. You can think of coal as "fossil wood."

Coal deposits are found all over the United States. The largest and best ones are in the eastern part of our country.

ICE

What is ice?

ICE IS THE colorless mineral that floats in water! Ice is really a water crystal, formed when the temperature of water or moisture in the air reaches the *freezing point,* indicated by 32° on the Fahrenheit thermometer or 0° on the centigrade thermometer.

Ice expands (increases its volume) as it forms. If one were to measure out eleven equal parts of water and freeze it, one would find that it takes up as much space as twelve parts. When there is no room for water to expand, pressure becomes strong — water pipes, for example, will often split open in winter.

Icebergs, being lighter than water, will float. In the sea about one-eighth of an iceberg is visible — the rest of it is hidden below the surface.

ASBESTOS

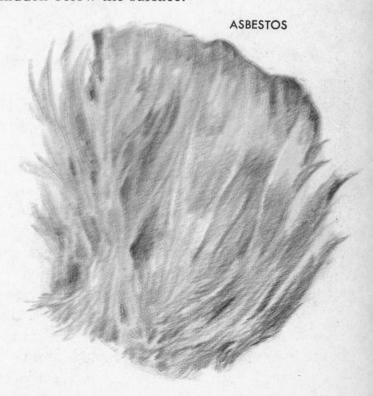

ASBESTOS

What is asbestos?

ASBESTOS is a mineral that does not burn! It is useful around stoves and hot places, for it will keep things near the stove from burning.

Asbestos is a light-colored mineral that comes from a kind of serpentine. It is made into asbestos cloth, asbestos paper and other helpful things. If you wore a pair of asbestos gloves, you could touch and handle hot things without getting burned!

START A ROCK AND MINERAL COLLECTION

How do you begin a rock and mineral collection? YOU will find it easy to start a rock and mineral collection. Begin to collect by looking near your home.

If you have a garden, you may find a rock there. If there is an open field close by, it should contain some rocks you will want to have in your collection.

Are workmen building a new house near your home? They may have dug up some rocks or minerals you do not have. Sometimes the builders bring in new kinds of rocks. Look them over.

There might be some you will want to collect, but ask permission first.

If you go into the country, watch for other new rocks or minerals. Look at new road cuts. This is often a good place to collect rocks. A dry creek or stream is another excellent place to look.

One of the finest places will be in a rock quarry. Here you are sure to find some worthwhile specimens. Of course, you must be careful to watch out for overhanging rocks or loose stones. It is well to collect with a partner — and more fun, too!

What will you need to collect rocks and minerals?

YOU WILL need something to put your specimens in when you find them. If you are collecting near home, a heavy paper bag will do. But put in only a few small rocks at a time.

Most collectors use a collecting bag made of strong cloth. It has a strap that goes over your shoulder to help carry heavy loads. Surplus goods stores usually have a bag of this kind.

You will often need to break off rocks and break open new ones. A hammer or even another stone will sometimes help. With a hammer, or a prospector's pick, you can chip off a small piece of rock from a larger one.

Rock and mineral collectors like to take home only one or two of each kind of rock they find. It does not help to take too many of each. You would soon run out of room in which to keep them.

How can you keep your rocks and minerals?

YOU WILL want to keep your best rocks and minerals. It will help if you keep each kind together. The igneous rocks can go into one box. All of the sedimentary and the metamorphic rocks should be put into other boxes.

Shoe boxes or wooden cigar boxes make good containers. A label on the outside of the box will help you to locate specimens quickly.

Each rock should be labeled separately before you put it into your collection bag. A good system is to put a piece of adhesive tape with a number on it on the sample. In your collecting notebook write the name of the specimen and where you found it. Later on, at home, paint a small round white spot on your specimen with white paint. India ink numbers over the white paint will show up fine.

Start your numbers with one, two, three, and so on. This will help you to keep your collection organized. Do not carelessly try to collect everything and put off labeling your rocks until later.

IDENTIFICATION CHART OF MAJOR SPECIMENS

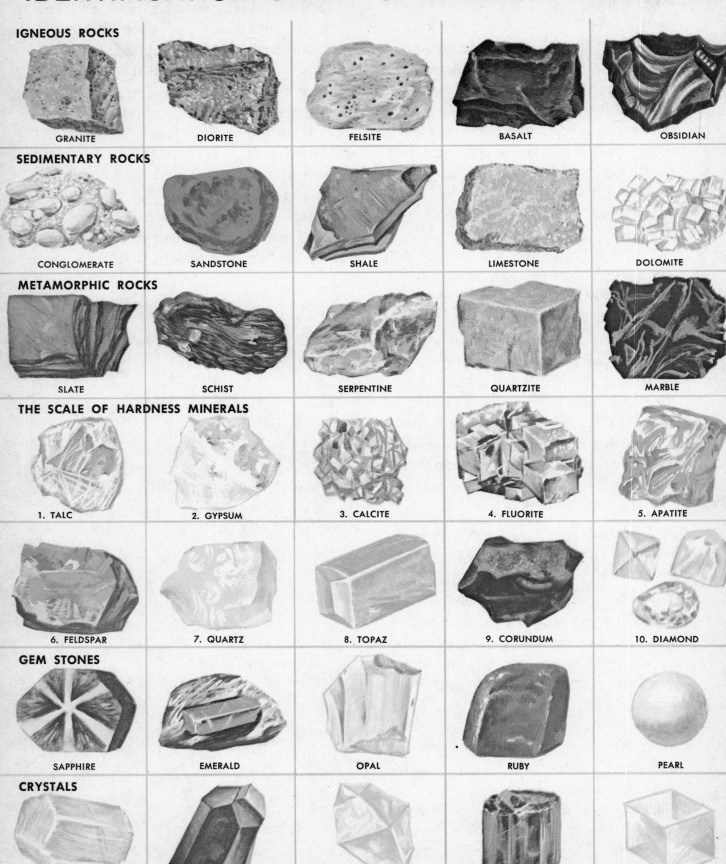

IGNEOUS ROCKS

GRANITE · DIORITE · FELSITE · BASALT · OBSIDIAN

SEDIMENTARY ROCKS

CONGLOMERATE · SANDSTONE · SHALE · LIMESTONE · DOLOMITE

METAMORPHIC ROCKS

SLATE · SCHIST · SERPENTINE · QUARTZITE · MARBLE

THE SCALE OF HARDNESS MINERALS

1. TALC · 2. GYPSUM · 3. CALCITE · 4. FLUORITE · 5. APATITE

6. FELDSPAR · 7. QUARTZ · 8. TOPAZ · 9. CORUNDUM · 10. DIAMOND

GEM STONES

SAPPHIRE · EMERALD · OPAL · RUBY · PEARL

CRYSTALS

AMAZONITE · EPIDOTE · SULPHUR · RUTILE · HALITE